Colourful Cushions in Needlepoint

20 Needlepoint Projects

Colourful Cushions in Needlepoint

20 Needlepoint Projects

Stella Edwards

B T Batsford Ltd, London

Acknowledgements

I would like to thank Susan Rockley, Louise McDermott, Pam Gardiner and my mother Margaret Edwards for helping me to make up the designs most beautifully.

Text, designs © Stella Edwards
The moral right of the author has been asserted.
Photographs, illustrations © B T Batsford

First published in 1997 by
B T Batsford Ltd
583 Fulham Road
London SW6 5BY

A catalogue record for this book is available from the British Library.

ISBN 0 7134 7996 5

Printed in Hong Kong

Photography by Shona Wood

except page 54 which is by Paul Bricknell
Colour illustrations by Carol Hill
Colour charts by Anthony Lawrence

Contents

Introduction

You can never have enough cushions scattered in your home and when they have been made by hand they will always be admired and treasured. Needlepoint cushions have a special quality of their own. I think that this unique quality is a result of the strong tones and the range of different colours to be found in yarns today. Needlepoint is also a most rewarding pastime. Not only is there the pleasure that comes from time spent making something beautiful, but there is also the satisfaction of seeing a finished article which can then be used for many years to come.

The art of embroidery can be traced to the Far East, back to around AD500, where it was passed from the Persians to the Greeks. The King of Pergamus is said to have been one of the first to have used gold thread, and the women of Sidon were renowned for their embroidery skill. Needlepoint is a form of embroidery in which stitches are used to cover an open canvas. Also known as canvas work embroidery, it became popular in the eighteenth century when ladies embroidered designs on canvas fabric using woven tapestries as an inspiration.

Tapestry has a longer history; this fabric woven on a jacquard loom was introduced to Europe by the Saracens in the twelfth century. In the Middle Ages, the Ile-de-France was the leading producer of tapestries, with Paris its undoubted capital. Then the systematic plundering of towns in the Hundred Years War sent the tapestry makers fleeing northwards to Arras where they founded the Ateliers d'Arras. Flanders then became an established centre for tapestry after Arras was pillaged by the Spaniards. This period saw the appearance of epic scenes in tapestry. Kings and Princes had tapestries woven of their tournaments, combats, victories and even their hunting parties. This period remains the most prolific for tapestries of unrivalled quality.

Tapestry took root in Flanders during the latter part of the twelfth century and was carried to various parts of Western Europe by the refugees who were driven from their fatherland by the tyranny of the Spaniards. With the Renaissance and the arrival of the Italian artists, tapestry radically changed style. A chief influence on tapestry design was Raphael who introduced order, clarity, and perspective to composition along with a rich decor which characterised the highly-coloured style of this period.

In France in 1660, the royal factory of Les Gobelins was established under the protection of Louis XIV and the highest class of tapestry was produced here. After the death of Louis XIV, the official formal subjects of tapestry weaving gave way to more imaginative and romantic subjects and included beautiful landscapes. The French Revolution put a stop to the creative genius of these tapestry specialists, but in 1795 three tapestry makers, Beauvais, Aubusson and Felletin reopened the factories and began to reproduce many of the great designs. This continued right up until the nineteenth century.

The history of tapestry not only shows the development of designs, as in the magnificent Mille Fleurs group with their splendid backgrounds of flowers, but also reveals the fashions of the time. The Mille Fleurs scenes became popular towards the end of the fifteenth century. One collection in the Mille Fleurs group is of six pieces called 'Les Dames à la Unicorne'. The tapestries represent the five senses and were woven as an engagement present. The various subjects are symbolic; the lion and unicorn bear the coat-of-arms and represent strength and purity and the organ in the design symbolises the sense of hearing. Over the centuries tapestry making techniques have changed. The jacquard loom was created by Joseph Marie Jacquard (1752-1854) and this piece of equipment is the basis of contemporary designs which retain the old look of these more ancient tapestries.

The art of needlepoint evolved from this long tradition of tapestry. In recent years needlepoint has enjoyed a huge revival in popularity and there is a wide and ever-increasing range of designs and projects to make, ranging from kits that come complete with the yarns to pre-printed canvases, to plain canvases from which you can work patterns and designs of your own choice.

The Medieval Rabbit and the Unicorn projects are both designs taken from old tapestries. Both are worked on a classic blue background and are surrounded by woodland flowers, symbols typical of the Mille Fleurs tapestries. The Sampler design also in this chapter was a challenge as samplers are traditionally stitched in cross stitch on beautiful linen fabric, but the result proves it can be done. Needlepoint is quite a coarse medium in which to work so it is necessary to remove detail, to prevent the design becoming muddled. However, you must keep a balance between interest and over detail, otherwise the design can become flat and uninteresting. There was no problem in choosing woollen yarns to match the original silks as there are so many colours available now.

Apart from the historical section, there are floral designs and designs for special occasions. Each section gave me a chance to explore different subjects and colours. All the designs here, whether square cushions, round cushions, rectangular cushions or pincushions, are functional items and should be seen, used and enjoyed. They are at their best stuffed to their fullest so they can make a real statement in your room – 'look at me and admire!' is what you want them to say! And I hope you will be inspired by the designs you see in this book and have the confidence to then have a go yourself.

Stella Edwards

Needlepoint is a form of canvas work embroidery in which the stitches entirely cover the material on which the work is done. Various stitches can be included under the term canvas work embroidery but needlepoint generally implies using a half cross stitch or tent stitch.

It is very important to work in good light and try to keep the tension of the threads the same throughout to give a professional finish. This either comes naturally right from the beginning or it may take you a while to perfect. Practise several rows of stitches on small pieces of canvas and try to keep the tension the same all the way through. Do not pull the yarn too tightly as the thread will not cover the holes and the canvas may begin to twist.

Materials and Techniques

Techniques

Starting and Finishing

Tying a knot in the yarn end is an easy way to start, but this is not the best way to work. Start by passing the needle down through the canvas about 2.5 cm (1 in) from where the first stitch is to be and leave a 10 cm (4 in) end. Hold this tight as you begin to stitch. After working the stitches, take the yarn end to the wrong side to finish, then pass the needle through the backs of the worked stitches. Finish the starting end by rethreading the needle with the 10 cm thread you allowed and passing it through the backs of the worked stitches in the same way.

Cutting Corners

After finishing the stitching of a pincushion or cushion, the corners of the canvas should be cut diagonally. This avoids building up a bulk of canvas in the corners after making up which could distort the finished work.

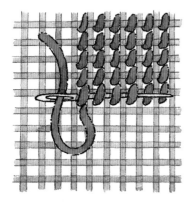

Pass the yarn end through the backs of the stitches.

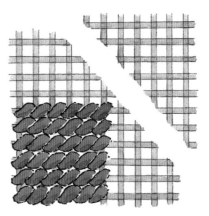

Cut the corners diagonally

Stretching the Finished Needlepoint

When the embroidery has been completed the canvas may be slightly askew. This is easily rectified by dampening it on the back with warm water (Fig. a), pinning it firmly to a board covered with a tea towel or piece of blotting paper (Fig. b) and allowing it to dry naturally. Be careful not to soak the needlepoint. When tugging it back into shape you can be quite firm with the embroidery and you will need to position the drawing pins about 1.5 cm (⅝ in) from each other. Press it quickly on the back with a hot steam iron, and the design should then be ready to make up. If the work is still distorted repeat the process.

Fig. a. Damp the canvas with warm water

Fig. b. Pin the canvas to a board which you have covered with a tea towel

Backing a Cushion

Backing a cushion is a simple process and if you do not have a sewing machine then hand stitching is equally suitable. The backing material you choose should be reasonably thick – I tend to use upholstery velvet which is readily available in a great variety of colours. You can use zips for attaching the opening and they will allow the cushion pad to be removed easily. Alternatively you can leave a gap at the bottom of a cushion, stitching it up after the cushion pad has been inserted.

When inserting a zip fastener you will need to cut two pieces of fabric. To calculate the size, divide the area of the stretched needlepoint in half widthwise and add about 1.5 cm (⅝ in) seam allowance all round to each piece. With right sides together, join at each end of the centre seam, leaving enough seam open in the middle for the length of the zip fastener. Pin and tack the zip fastener into position and stitch it using a sewing machine with a zip foot or by hand using backstitch.

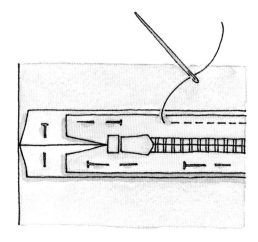

Both cord and piping sewn to the edge of a cushion make a simple but effective finish. There is so much choice available that you need to be careful to select a cord that will enhance the design rather than detract from it.

Stitches

Half Cross Stitch

This stitch can be worked either from right to left or from left to right. It is important to ensure that all the stitches slope in the same direction on the front of the canvas. On the back you should see short vertical stitches.

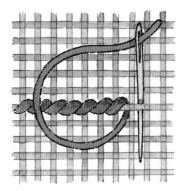

Tent Stitch

This is a more hard-wearing stitch as it completely covers the canvas, as opposed to the half cross stitch which, in effect, only covers the face of the embroidery. However it does use more yarn (sometimes up to a third more) which should be noted when buying materials for a design.

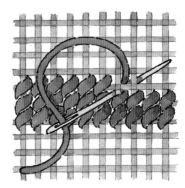

Cross Stitch

This stitch forms a cross on the front of the design. Work a row of half cross stitches and then work back in the opposite direction. When mixing half cross and cross stitches in one design I make the top cross stitch run in the opposite direction to the rest of the half cross stitches for maximum effect.

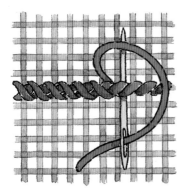

French Knot

This stitch is very easy to do, although getting the right tension may need some practise. Bring the yarn to the front of the canvas in the required position, hold it down with your thumb, encircle it with the needle and pull through. Then insert the needle back through the canvas behind the knot.

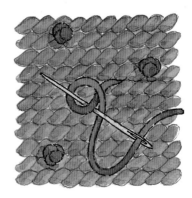

Long-Armed Cross Stitch

I have used this decorative stitch to join the fronts and backs of pincushions. It is similar to cross stitch but the 'crosses' are worked closer together and with a longer top stitch, leaving no canvas showing. You need to work two holes forwards, and one hole back.

Rice Stitch

This is also known as the 'crossed corners stitch' which describes it perfectly. First, stitch an area of large cross stitches (usually worked over four holes in the canvas) in one colour. Then work smaller stitches in each of the corners of the large stitches as shown in the diagram. Use a contrasting colour.

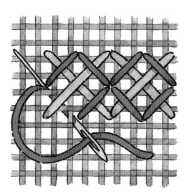

Whipped Chain Stitch

This decorative stitch is used to disguise the edging of the Butterfly Cushion. First, sew a chain stitch. Do not pull the stitches too tightly as this will spoil the characteristic chain-like appearance. With the same, or a contrasting coloured yarn, work the needle from right to left under one of the chains. Then work it over to the next chain, again from right to left. Go under each chain, remembering not to pull the thread too tightly.

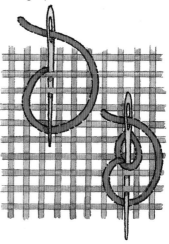

Back Stitch

This is one of the basic embroidery stitches and is very useful when highlighting areas of similar colours, or for outlining. Remember not to pull the working thread too tightly as this will make holes between the stitches. Work it over one hole, as shown below.

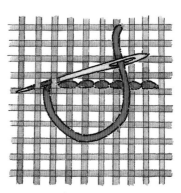

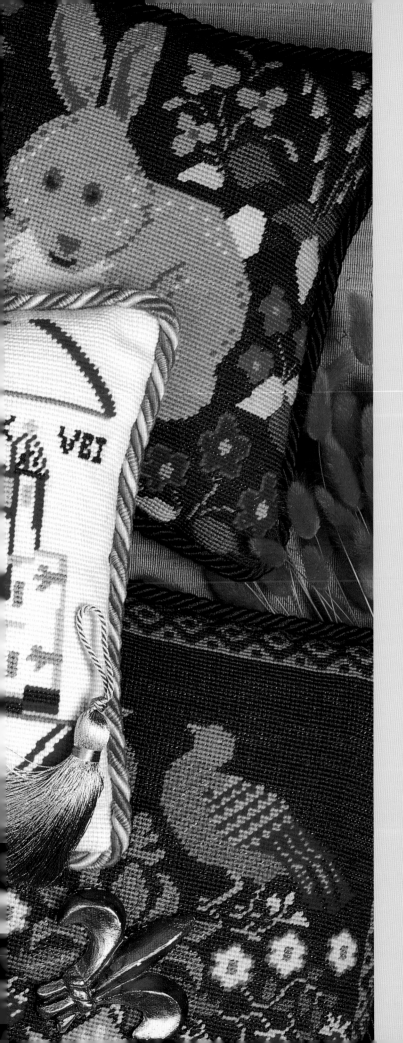

There are so many periods in history with inspiring designs to interpret in needlepoint that it was difficult to select just a few. Those that I have chosen incorporate a wide range of images: the little Medieval rabbit, the unicorn inspired by the famous Mille Fleurs tapestries, the sampler design, a scene from the Bayeux Tapestry, a classic William Morris design and a woodland scene designed from an archive Joie de Vivre textile.

The two most challenging designs were those used for the Sampler and the Bayeux Tapestry cushions. They were both originally worked in fine silk on linen and so they needed to be simplified to suit the coarser medium of wool on canvas. These finished cushions successfully retain the 'feel' of the original pieces.

Historical Designs

Medieval Rabbit Cushion

This charming little rabbit was taken from the famous Mille Fleurs range of tapestries which depict rural scenes overflowing with country freshness and charm. On these, gentle ladies, lords and peasant folk frolic on a background of 'bord de Loire' flowers, all in muted soft-toned colours. Various rabbits, along with antelopes, foxes, dogs, birds and squirrels were woven with a multitude of flowers to form a distinctive and elegant background to the central design. I chose this particular rabbit as he looked so happy!

Materials

Anchor tapisserie wool:
    1 skein 9442
    1 skein 8264
    1 skein 8734
    1 skein 9076
    1· skein 9006
    1 skein 9172
    2 skeins 9556
    3 skeins 9524
    7 skeins 8740
One piece of 10 hole double thread canvas
    size 40.5 x 40.5 cm (16 x 16 in)
Backing fabric
Cushion pad size 30 cm (12 in) square
Cord

Instructions

1   Follow the chart to work the design. Start from the middle and use half cross stitch throughout.

2   Press the embroidery on the back with a hot steam iron over a damp cloth and gently pull it back into shape.

3   With the right sides together, sew the backing fabric to the embroidery, starting one third along the bottom edge of the cushion. Sew around the four sides, leaving a large gap to allow the cushion pad to go in. Trim the excess canvas and fabric.

4   Turn the cushion right side out.

5   Stuff with a cushion pad and carefully sew up the gap, leaving a smaller gap of 5 cm (2 in).

6   Sew the cord around the edge of the cushion, starting and finishing at the small gap. This will hide the ends of the cord and give a neat finish.

Key

Anchor tapisserie wool:

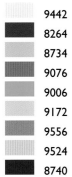

	9442
	8264
	8734
	9076
	9006
	9172
	9556
	9524
	8740

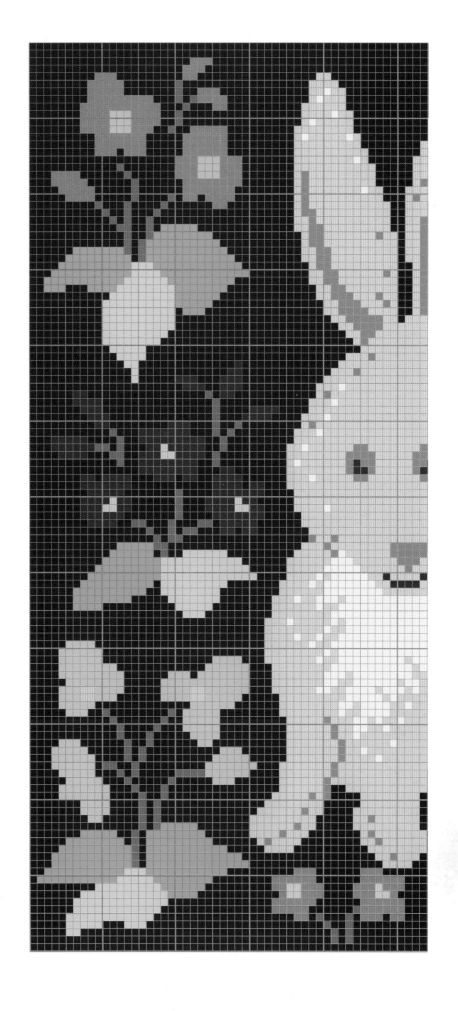

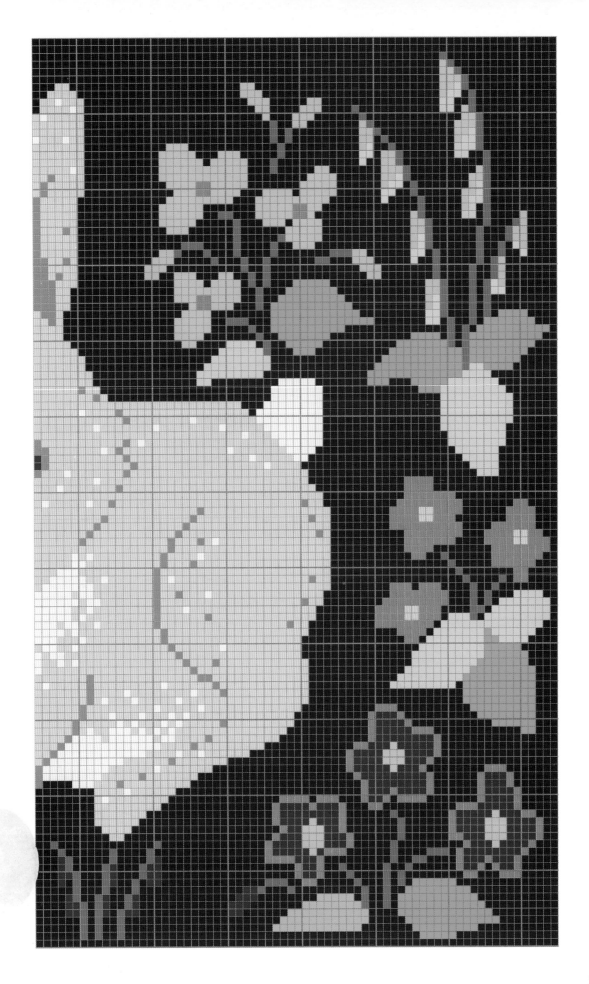

Bayeux Tapestry Cushion

The Bayeux Tapestry is a pictorial history of the invasion of England by the Normans, beginning with King Harold's visit to the Norman court and ending with his death at the battle of Hastings in 1066. It is thought to have been the work of Matilda, the wife of William the Conqueror and it is 65 m (214 feet) long and only 51 cm (20 in) wide. Although called a tapestry it is, in fact, a good example of fine embroidery sewn onto linen.

I have chosen a scene from the very beginning of the Tapestry for this cushion. Note that hands and faces are very difficult to interpret in canvas work embroidery so I have sewn them here in stranded cotton using two threads and then stitched facial details with black cotton sewing thread.

Materials

Anchor tapisserie wool:
  1 skein 9018
  1 skein 9100
  1 skein 8156
  1 skein 8612
  1 skein 9022
  1 skein 9646
  1 skein 8136
  1 skein 8164
  2 skeins 8218
  12 skeins 8036
Anchor stranded cotton:
  1 skein 0880
One piece of 10 hole double thread canvas
  size 51 × 40.5 cm (20 × 16 in)
Backing fabric
Cushion pad size 30 × 40 cm (12 × 15¾ in)
Cord

Instructions

1   Follow the chart to work the design, starting from the middle. Use half cross stitch throughout.

2   Press the embroidery on the back with a hot steam iron over a damp cloth and gently pull it back into shape.

3   With the right sides together, sew the backing fabric to the embroidery, starting one third along the bottom edge of the cushion. Sew around the four sides, leaving a large gap to allow the cushion pad to go in. Trim the excess canvas and fabric.

4   Turn the cushion right side out.

5   Stuff with a cushion pad and carefully sew up the gap, leaving a smaller gap of 5 cm (2 in).

6   Sew the cord around the edge of the cushion, starting and finishing at the small gap. This will hide the ends of the cord and give a neat finish.

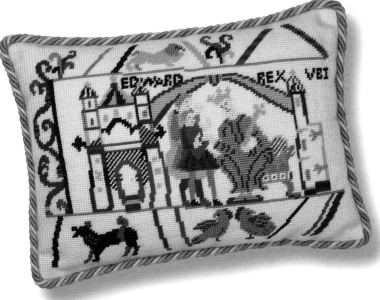

Key

Anchor tapisserie wool:

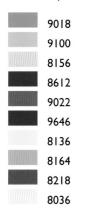

9018
9100
8156
8612
9022
9646
8136
8164
8218
8036

Anchor stranded cotton:

0880

Unicorn Cushion

The Unicorn motif is a symbol of purity and is found in many medieval tapestries. Towards the end of the fifteenth century, the Val de Loire became a popular place for tapestry makers and it was in this 'cradle of French kings' that the most prestigious works were made, including the Les Mille Fleurs range.

Tapestries were regarded as immensely valuable items, which is not surprising as they were laborious and time-consuming to weave, using threads dyed from natural plant extracts. Noblemen used to take them on their travels from castle to castle and when they went away to war the tapestries often became part of the victor's spoils. Some tapestries changed hands several times in this way!

Materials

Anchor tapisserie wool:
  1 skein 8734
  1 skein 8264
  1 skein 8218
  1 skein 9524
  1 skein 8016
  1 skein 9594
  2 skeins 9556
  2 skeins 9172
  2 skeins 9076
  2 skeins 9006
  3 skeins 8036
  12 skeins 8740
One piece of 10 hole double thread canvas
  size 48 × 48 cm (19 × 19 in)
Backing fabric
Cushion pad size 40 cm (15¾ in) square
Cord

Instructions

1 Follow the chart to work the design, starting from the middle. Use half cross stitch throughout.

2 Press the embroidery on the back with a hot steam iron over a damp cloth and gently pull it back into shape.

3 With the right sides together, sew the backing fabric to the embroidery, starting one third of the way along the bottom edge of the cushion. Sew around the four sides, leaving a large gap to allow the cushion pad to go in. Trim the excess canvas and fabric.

4 Turn the cushion right side out.

5 Stuff with a cushion pad and carefully sew up the gap leaving a smaller gap of 5 cm (2 in).

6 Sew the cord around the edge of the cushion starting and finishing at the small gap. This will hide the ends of the cord and give a neat finish.

Key

Anchor tapisserie wool:

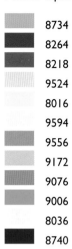

8734
8264
8218
9524
8016
9594
9556
9172
9076
9006
8036
8740

Sampler Cushion

Sampler designs are usually worked in full cross stitch on linen, so interpreting original samplers into needlepoint was quite a challenge. This design is taken from an original English sampler created in 1785 by Elizabeth Brain. She used a woollen canvas with coloured silks and a variety of stitches including chain, cross, tent, stem, long and short, satin overcast and eyelet.

I have left a gap across the top of the work where originally there was the alphabet, numbers and the creator's name. You can easily sew in your own name by oversewing the woollen threads with stranded cotton in a suitable contrasting colour.

Materials

Anchor tapisserie wool:

1 skein 8056	2 skeins 8036
1 skein 8062	2 skeins 9180
1 skein 9682	2 skeins 9006
1 skein 9018	2 skeins 9076
1 skein 8302	2 skeins 8136
1 skein 8396	2 skeins 9098
1 skein 8686	9 skeins 8006
1 skein 9450	

One piece of 10 hole double thread canvas size 51 × 40.5 cm (20 × 16 in)
Backing fabric
Cushion pad size 30 × 40 cm (12 × 15¾ in)
Cord

Instructions

1 Follow the chart to work the design, starting from the middle and using mainly half cross stitch. The two deer, the yellow and pink birds and the little chair under the tree should be worked in a full cross stitch with the top of the cross stitch running in the opposite direction to the rest of the work. This technique allows them to stand out from the rest of the design.

2 Press the embroidery on the back with a hot steam iron over a damp cloth and gently pull it back into shape.

3 With the right sides together, sew the backing fabric to the embroidery, starting one third of the way along the bottom edge of the cushion. Sew around the four sides, leaving a large gap to allow the cushion pad to go in. Trim the excess canvas and fabric.

4 Turn the cushion right side out.

5 Stuff with a cushion pad and carefully sew up the gap, leaving a smaller gap of 5 cm (2 in).

6 Sew the cord around the edge of the cushion, starting and finishing at the small gap. This will hide the ends of the cord and give a neat finish.

Key

Anchor tapisserie wool:

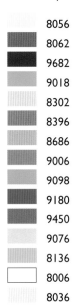

	8056
	8062
	9682
	9018
	8302
	8396
	8686
	9006
	9098
	9180
	9450
	9076
	8136
	8006
	8036

William Morris Cushion

This design was inspired by one of William Morris' most popular textile designs, Strawberry Thief, printed in about 1883. William Morris was a poet, painter, philanthropist and designer who died in 1896. Virtually single-handedly he changed British taste from the dark clutter of the Victorian period to the fresh, flowing lines of the Arts and Crafts Movement which then evolved into the Art Nouveau style. He was very much against the use of the crude chemical dyes of the time and experimented with historic dyes to create the strong, subtle and resonant colours that are now associated with William Morris – especially the colour indigo which took him a decade to perfect.

Materials

Anchor tapisserie wool:
  1 skein 9556
  1 skein 9524
  1 skein 9172
  1 skein 8112
  1 skein 8218
  1 skein 9006
  1 skein 9076
  3 skeins 8920
  7 skeins 8740
One piece of 10 hole double thread canvas
  size 48 × 48 cm (19 × 19 in)
Backing fabric
Cushion pad size 38 cm (15 in)
Cord

Instructions

1   Follow the chart to work the design, starting from the middle. Use half cross stitch throughout.

2   Press the embroidery on the back with a hot steam iron over a damp cloth and gently pull it back into shape.

3   With the right sides together, sew the backing fabric to the embroidery, starting one third along the bottom edge of the cushion. Sew around the four sides, leaving a large gap to allow the cushion pad to go in. Trim the excess canvas and fabric.

4   Turn the cushion right side out.

5   Stuff with a cushion pad and carefully sew up the gap leaving a smaller gap of 5 cm (2 in).

6   Sew the cord around the edge of the cushion starting and finishing at the small gap. This will hide the cord ends and give a neat finish.

Key

Anchor tapisserie wool:

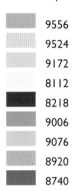

	9556
	9524
	9172
	8112
	8218
	9006
	9076
	8920
	8740

Woodland Scene Cushion

This design featuring two women dressed in medieval clothes is nostalgic and full of movement. It is very hard to get the correct look of skin with tapestries incorporating figures. I think this is because it is difficult to create the soft gradations of skin tone with woollen yarns on this scale. After much experimentation I found stranded cotton a much gentler medium to use. I have highlighted the two girls' faces using sewing cotton and used a brown stranded cotton to create the shoes.

Materials

Anchor tapisserie wool:

1 skein 9510	1 skein 9098
1 skein 9642	2 skeins 9006
1 skein 8058	2 skeins 9492
1 skein 9524	2 skeins 8036
1 skein 9638	3 skeins 9076
1 skein 9022	3 skeins 9014
1 skein 8734	4 skeins 9018
1 skein 8990	8 skeins 8740
1 skein 8602	short length of 8264

Anchor stranded cotton:
  1 skein 0880
  1 skein 0359
One piece of 10 hole double thread canvas
  size 50 × 50 cm (20 × 20 in)
Backing fabric
Cushion pad size 40 cm (15¾ in) square
Cord

Instructions

1 Follow the chart to work the design starting from the middle. Use half cross stitch throughout. When working the girls' arms, legs and faces use a double yarn of the stranded cotton in the needle. Work the faces using a single thread of stranded cotton, but two threads for the shoes.

2 Press the embroidery on the back with a hot steam iron over a damp cloth and gently pull it back into shape.

3 With the right sides together, sew the backing fabric to the embroidery, starting one third of the way along the bottom edge of the cushion. Sew around the four sides, leaving a large gap to allow the cushion pad to go in. Trim back any excess canvas and fabric, cutting the corners at an angle.

4 Turn the cushion right side out.

5 Stuff with a cushion and sew the gap together leaving a smaller gap of 5 cm (2 in)

6 Stitch the cord around the edges of the cushion starting and finishing at the small gap. This will hide the ends of the cord and give a neat finish.

Key

Anchor tapisserie wool:

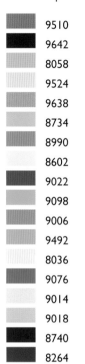

	9510
	9642
	8058
	9524
	9638
	8734
	8990
	8602
	9022
	9098
	9006
	9492
	8036
	9076
	9014
	9018
	8740
	8264

Anchor stranded cotton:

	0359
	0880

The immense variety of flowers makes it difficult to decide upon those from which to draw ideas for floral designs. I have a few particular favourites which I made a point of including here. The distinctive red of poppies will always brighten an interior. I have used this flower in a square cushion and in the floral bolster. Another favourite is the pansy which you can find throughout the year in a wide spectrum of colours and is included as a small pincushion design. The sunflower features in another cushion where I combined different stitches to give a richer texture – rice stitch was used around the border and a number of French knots were incorporated. Other flowers include the herbs camomile and lavender, as well as primroses, pinks, forget-me-nots and simple wild marsh flowers.

Flower Designs

Pansy Pincushion

Pansies are one of my favourite flowers to stitch. There are so many varieties of pansy nowadays that any mix of colours will look stunning. The colours are always strong, with blues, yellows, purples and black being the main combinations I associate them with, although paler violets and powder blues are common, along with striking bright reds and oranges. I have created a different design for the back of the pincushion with little pansy flowerbuds which looks very pretty. This is a small project that is quick to make and would be ideal as a gift to be used time and time again.

Materials

Anchor tapisserie wool:
    I skein 8524
    I skein 8592
    I skein 8490
    I skein 9004
    I skein 8992
    I skein 8136
    I skein 8016
    3 skeins 9800
Two pieces of 12 hole interlock canvas
   size 18 × 18 cm (7 × 7 in)
Polyester toy stuffing

Instructions

1   Follow the charts to work the designs, starting from the middle of each. Use half cross stitch throughout.

2   Press the embroideries on the back with a hot steam iron over a damp cloth and gently pull them back into shape.

3   Trim back the canvas, cutting the corners at an angle.

4   Fold the unworked canvas to the wrong side. Hold the front and back edges together with right sides on the outside. Stitch the two pieces of the canvas together with a long-armed cross stitch, starting one third of the way along the bottom edge. Work around the four sides using long-armed cross stitch. Leave a gap of about 4 cm (1½in).

5   Stuff the pincushion with the polyester toy stuffing.

6   Sew up the gap with long-armed cross stitch.

Key

Anchor tapisserie wool:

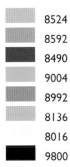

8524
8592
8490
9004
8992
8136
8016
9800

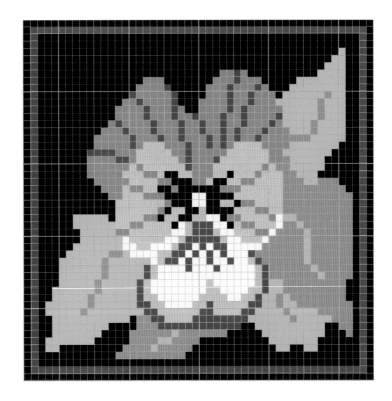

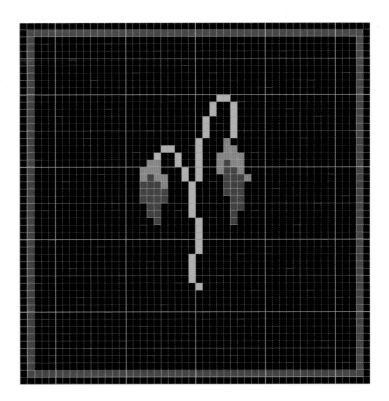

Herbal Cushion

Lavender is known for its soothing, relaxing and stress-reducing properties. It has a long history – it is said that the Greeks and Romans used lavender to make perfumes and ointments. It is a traditional cottage-garden plant with its grey-green spiky foliage and spires of mauvy-blue flowers providing colour throughout the year. It is native to Mediterranean countries, especially in the sun-baked Maquis region of southern France where it grows in profusion.

When you add the stuffing to this cushion also add a lavender sachet. Make this by taking two pieces of muslin or loose cotton and sewing around three sides. Turn the material inside out, stuff with dried lavender and sew up the gap.

Materials

Anchor tapisserie wool:
   1 skein 8602
   1 skein 9006
   1 skein 9004
   1 skein 8112
   1 skein 8606
   1 skein 8612
   1 skein 9022
   1 skein 9076
   1 skein 9598
   1 skein 9618
   4 skeins 8006
One piece of 12 hole interlock fabric
   size 33 x 33 cm (13 x 13 in)
Backing fabric
Polyester toy stuffing
Sachet of dried lavender
Cord

Instructions

1   Follow the chart to work the design, starting from the middle. Use half cross stitch throughout.

2   Press the embroidery on the back with a hot steam iron over a damp cloth and gently pull it back into shape.

3   With the right sides together, sew the backing fabric to the embroidery, starting one third of the way along the bottom edge of the cushion. Sew around the four sides, leaving a large gap to allow the cushion pad to go in. Trim back any excess canvas and fabric, cutting the corners at an angle.

4   Turn the cushion right side out.

5   Stuff the cushion with the polyester toy stuffing, adding the herbal sachet.

6   Sew the gap together, leaving a small gap of about 2.5 cm (1 in).

7   Sew the cord around the edge of the cushion, starting and finishing at the small gap.

Key

Anchor tapisserie wool:

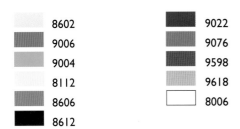

8602	9022
9006	9076
9004	9598
8112	9618
8606	8006
8612	

Wild Flowers Bolster

Forget-me-nots, primroses, pinks and poppies are some of the flowers which have been put together to create this colourful design for a bolster cushion. Although I have chosen strong, vibrant colours and placed them on a black background, any mixture of colours could be used, especially those that enhance your interior decoration. I have added some butterflies and ladybirds and then stitched two rows of little ladybirds to run adjacent to the joining seam. This bolster is bright and cheerful, will look splendid anywhere, and would make an ideal headrest if soothing herbs were added in a sachet to the cushion padding. Try a combination of camomile and lavender.

To finish the bolster I have covered two buttons with one of the green yarns found in the design.

Materials

Anchor tapisserie wool:

I skein 8434	2 skeins 8202
I skein 8016	2 skeins 8006
I skein 8152	2 skeins 9094
I skein 8606	2 skeins 9002
I skein 9450	2 skeins 9098
I skein 8644	3 skeins 9120
2 skeins 8392	20 skeins of 9800

One piece of 10 hole double thread canvas size 63.5 x 63.5 cm (25 x 25 in)
Two pieces of 12 hole interlock canvas size 5 cm (2 in) square
Cushion pad size 45 x 17 cm (17¾ x 6¾ in) diameter
Herbal sachet (optional)
20 cm x 1.1 m (8 x 43¼ in) black velvet
Two buttons

Instructions

1 Follow the chart to work the design, starting in the middle. Use half cross-stitch throughout.

2 Press the embroidery on the back with a hot steam iron over a damp cloth and gently pull it back into shape.

3 Cut two strips of velvet 10 x 55 cm (4 x 21⅝ in) long. Turn over one long edge to make a hem and stitch the other to the needlepoint.

4 Pin the two edges of the embroidery together and sew either using a long-armed cross stitch to give a slightly raised finish, or carefully slip stitching them together with cotton thread. Sew the velvet widths together with cotton thread and trim any excess canvas and velvet.

5 Stuff the bolster with the cushion pad. Add a herbal sachet if desired.

6 Gather the ends of the velvet and sew them firmly in place.

7 Using the green 9120 on the 12 hole canvas, stitch enough rows to cover one button. Repeat for the other button.

8 Sew the buttons on each end.

Key

Anchor tapisserie wool:

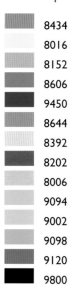

	8434
	8016
	8152
	8606
	9450
	8644
	8392
	8202
	8006
	9094
	9002
	9098
	9120
	9800

Butterfly Cushion

This beautiful round cushion depicts the splendid Swallowtail butterfly common to Europe and Asia. Typical of butterflies, the Swallowtail does most of its eating early in life as a caterpillar and shows a marked preference for milk parsley leaves, hence their inclusion on the design. It may live for over half a year as a caterpillar but survives less than a month as a butterfly. The bright-winged adult's purpose in life is to find a mate and breed, and having done this, its life is effectively over.

Materials

Anchor tapisserie wool:
    1 skein 8114
    1 skein 9172
    1 skein 8612
    1 skein 9534
    1 skein 9800
    1 skein 9646
    2 skeins 8038
    5 skeins 8006
    14 skeins 9018
One piece of 10 hole double thread canvas
    size 43 × 43 cm (17 × 17 in)
Two pieces of 10 hole double thread canvas
    size 61 × 12.5 cm (24 × 5 in)
Backing fabric
Cushion pad size 30 cm (12 in) diameter × 5 cm
    (12 in) depth

Instructions

1   Follow the charts to work the designs starting from the middle for the butterfly. Use half cross stitch throughout.

2   Press the pieces of embroidery on the back with a hot steam iron over a damp cloth and gently pull them back into shape.

3   Sew the side pieces to the top piece using sewing thread.

4   Sew the side pieces together again using sewing thread and trim any excess canvas.

5   Turn the work inside out and sew the backing fabric to the embroidery, leaving a gap for the cushion pad. Trim any excess canvas and fabric.

6   Turn the cushion right side out.

7   Stuff with a cushion pad and carefully sew up the gap.

8   Disguise the joins by working a neat chain stitch with the green background yarn around the top edge and the two seams down the sides. With either the same coloured yarn or a contrasting colour, loop the yarn over each chain to neatly raise the stitch and give a professional finish.

Key

Anchor tapisserie wool:

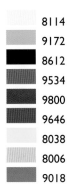

	8114
	9172
	8612
	9534
	9800
	9646
	8038
	8006
	9018

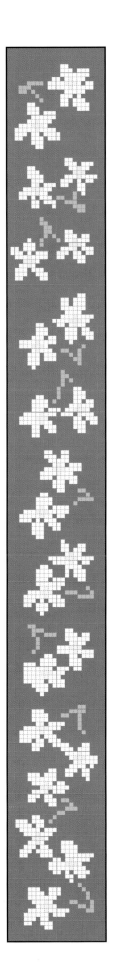

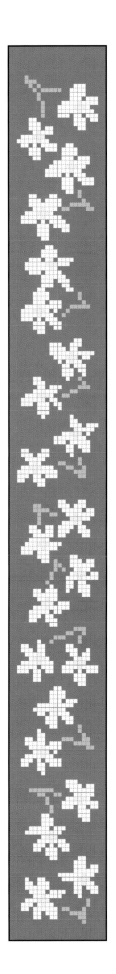

Poppies Cushion

The bright red of the poppy makes a vivid splash of colour against the golds and yellows of farmers' ripening crops. Nowadays this view is rarer and the poppy struggles to survive in an intensively farmed countryside. The most well-known poppy is the common field poppy. This was a particular favourite during the Art Nouveau period and appeared in opulent full bloom on a host of decorative articles. In this needlepoint design I have stitched the central panel and then mounted it on black velvet. As well as making a larger cushion, the depth of the velvet lifts the design to create a most striking effect.

Materials

Anchor tapisserie wool:
  1 skein 9180
  1 skein 9120
  1 skein 8486
  1 skein 8606
  1 skein 9800
  3 skeins 8052
  3 skeins 8202
  4 skeins 9100
One piece of 10 hole double thread canvas
  size 35.5 x 35.5 cm (14 x 14 in)
Black velvet to mount the needlepoint
Backing fabric
Cushion pad size 38 cm (15 in) square
Cord

Instructions

1 Follow the chart to work the design, starting from the middle. Use half cross stitch throughout.

2 Press the embroidery on the back with a hot steam iron over a damp cloth and gently pull it back into shape.

3 With the right sides together, sew the front fabric and the backing fabric together. Leave a gap for the cushion pad and trim off any excess fabric.

4 Turn the cushion right side out.

5 Trim the excess canvas around the edges of the needlepoint and turn to the back of the work.

6 Very carefully sew the embroidery to the front fabric ensuring no canvas shows.

7 Stuff with a cushion pad and carefully sew up the gap, leaving a smaller gap of 5 cm (2 in).

8 Sew the cord around the edge of the cushion, starting and finishing at the small gap. This will hide the ends of the cord and give a neat finish.

63

Key

Anchor tapisserie wool:

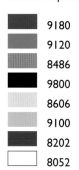

	9180
	9120
	8486
	9800
	8606
	9100
	8202
	8052

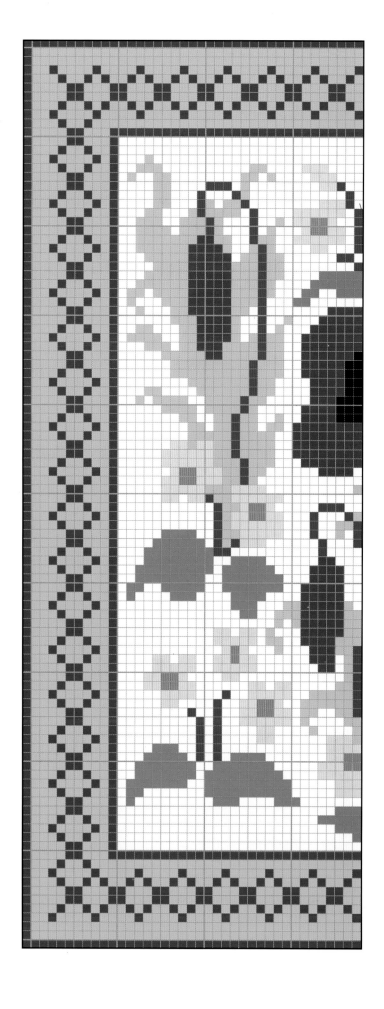

Sunflower Cushion

This is one of my favourite designs and it was great fun to stitch as there are a number of different stiches. French knots in yellow were used in the centre of each little green square and in the middle of the sunflower. A rice stitch was used in the yellow border and a cross stitch in brown in the centre. These give a good texture to the design, enhancing the actual sunflower. Sunflowers are believed to be native to Mexico and Peru and were introduced to Europe at about the end of the sixteenth century. They grow to a great height and follow the sun throughout the day giving an appearance of smiling faces.

Materials

Anchor tapisserie wool:
  1 skein 8152
  1 skein 9562
  1 skein 9602
  3 skeins 9018
  4 skeins 8016
  4 skeins 9022
  6 skeins 8136
One piece of 10 hole double thread canvas size
  48 × 48 cm (19 × 19 in)
Backing fabric
Cushion pad size 40 cm (15¾ in) square
Cord

Instructions

1 Follow the chart to work the design. Work cross stitches, French knots and a border of rice stitch as shown. Work all other areas in half cross stitch.

2 Press the embroidery on the back with a hot steam iron over a damp cloth and gently pull it back into shape.

3 With the right sides together, sew the backing fabric to the embroidery, starting one third of the way along the bottom edge of the cushion. Sew around the four sides leaving a large gap to allow the cushion pad to go in.

4 Trim back any excess canvas and fabric, cutting the corners at an angle.

5 Turn the cushion right side out.

6 Stuff with a cushion pad and sew the gap together, leaving a smaller gap of about 2.5 cm (1 in).

7 Stitch the cord around the edge of the cushion, starting and finishing at the small gap.

Key

Anchor tapisserie wool:

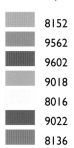

	8152
	9562
	9602
	9018
	8016
	9022
	8136

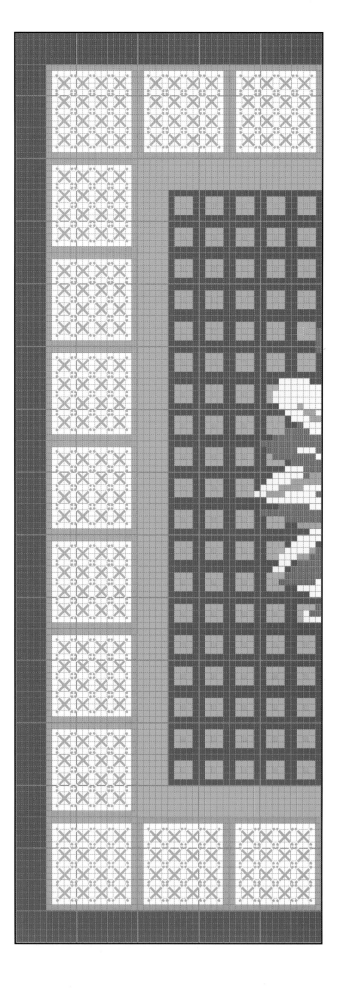

There is always a special occasion to be marked with a memorable gift, whether it be an anniversary, birthday, wedding, Christening or just a 'thank you'. I have created some ideas here which are quick and easy to stitch.

Most of the designs can be adapted to suit a particular person. The Baby Mobile, for example, could have the name of the baby embroidered down one side and perhaps the date of birth stitched on the other. The colours in the Bridal Cushion can be changed to co-ordinate with the colours worn by the bridesmaids and flowers and a ribbon loop can be added so the bride can carry it to the altar.

Wedding Pot Pourri Sachet

This delightful pot pourri sachet has been made with the bride in mind. After the wedding ceremony it is traditional to give the bride lucky horseshoes in silver and I thought this would make a splendid alternative. I have left the space in the middle of the heart blank as the initials of the bride and groom could be added using stranded cotton or a silver thread. The sachet is a simple design to create but effective and very original.

Materials

Anchor tapisserie wool:
  I skein 8526
  I skein 8394
  I skein 8396
  I skein 9096
  2 skeins 8006
I reel gold diadem thread 300
One piece of 12 hole interlock canvas
  size 23 × 23 cm (9 × 9 in)
Backing fabric
Polyester toy stuffing
Cord

Instructions

1   Follow the chart to work the design, starting from the middle. Use half cross stitch throughout.

2   Press the embroidery on the back with a hot steam iron over a damp cloth and gently pull it back into shape.

3   With the right sides together, sew the backing fabric to the embroidery leaving a gap for the stuffing. Trim the excess canvas and fabric.

4   Turn the cushion right side out.

5   Stuff with the polyester toy stuffing and sew up the gap, leaving a smaller gap at the top in the centre.

6   Sew the cord around the edge of the cushion, starting and finishing at the small gap. This will hide the ends of the cord and give a neat finish.

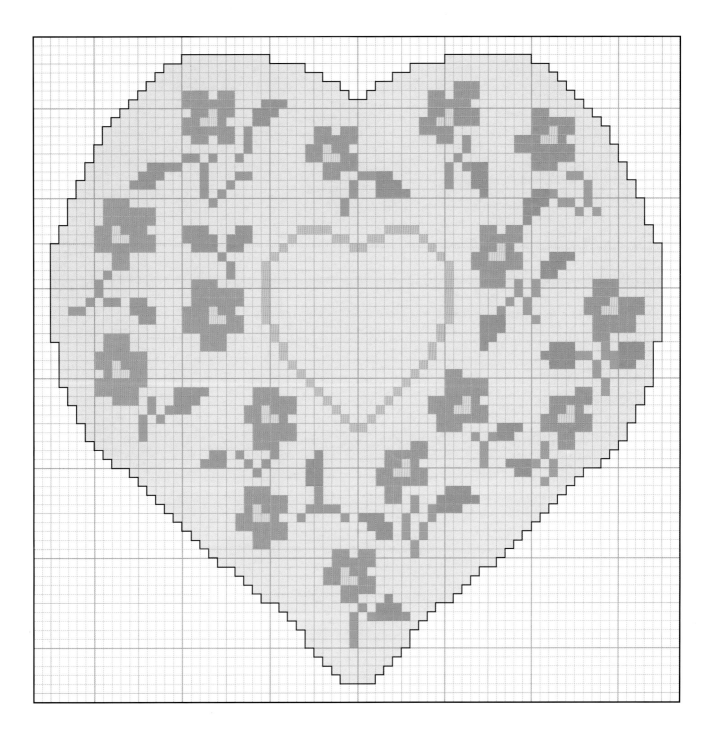

Key

Anchor tapisserie wool:

8526	
8394	
8396	
9096	
8006	

Gold diadem 300

Baby Mobile

A colourful mobile is such fun to have in a baby's room and this design is so simple it will be very quick to stitch. I have stitched a pink background on one side and blue on the other so that the cushion can be prepared in advance of a baby's birth! Alternatively you could introduce a background colour of your own choice.

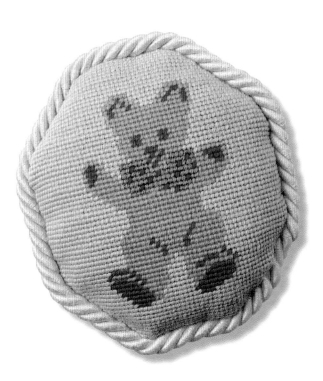

Materials

Anchor tapisserie wool:
    I skein 8392
    I skein 8782
    I skein 9524
    short length of 9560
    short length of 9100
    short length of 8202
One piece of 10 hole double thread canvas
    size 20 × 20 cm (8 × 8 in)
Polyester toy stuffing
Cord

Instructions

1 Follow the chart to work the designs, starting from the middle. Use half cross stitch throughout.

2 Press the pieces of embroidery on the back with a hot steam iron over a damp cloth and gently pull them back into shape.

3 With the right sides together, sew the front and back together, leaving a gap along one edge.

4 Trim back any excess canvas.

5 Turn the cushion right side out.

6 Stuff with the polyester toy stuffing and sew up the gap, leaving a smaller gap of about 2.5 cm (I in).

7 Stitch the cord around the edge of the cushion, starting and finishing at the small gap. Attach a ribbon to the top of the finished piece in a loop.

Key

Anchor tapisserie wool:

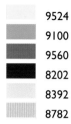

9524
9100
9560
8202
8392
8782

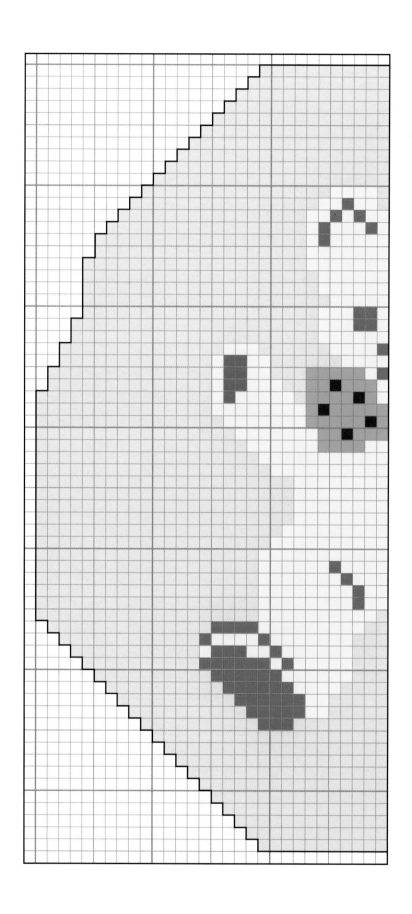

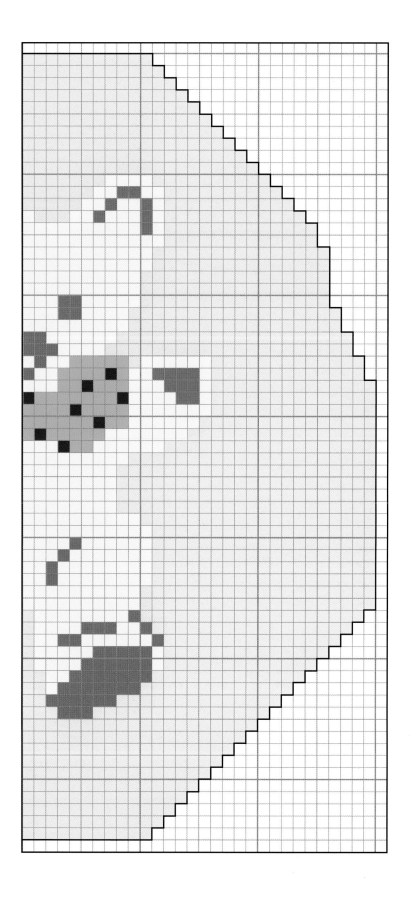

Sun Pincushion

It was Copernicus who asserted that the Sun regulates the movements of the planets and was the centre of our system rather than Earth. The Sun is a symbol of strength and warmth and a powerful decorative motif. In this needlepoint design I have given the Sun a cheerful face and used gold thread on the front and back to give it an extra sparkle.

Materials

Anchor tapisserie wool:
    1 skein 8016
    1 skein 8136
    3 skeins 8634
    short length of 9536
1 reel gold diadem thread 300
Two pieces of 12 hole interlock fabric size
    18 x 18 cm (7 x 7 in)
Polyester toy stuffing

Instructions

1 Follow the charts to work the designs, starting from the middle of each. Use half cross stitch throughout. When using the gold, use double thread in the needle.

2 Press the pieces of embroidery on the back with a hot steam iron over a damp cloth and gently pull them back into shape. Cut out each embroidery, ensuring the corners are cut at an angle.

3 Fold the unworked canvas to the wrong side. Hold the front and back edges together with right sides on the outside and, using long-armed cross stich, stitch the two pieces of the canvas together, starting one third along the bottom edge and working around the four sides. Leave a small gap for the stuffing.

4 Stuff the pincushion with the toy stuffing and close the gap with long-armed cross stitch.

Key

Anchor tapisserie wool:

8016

8634

9536

8136

Gold diadem 300

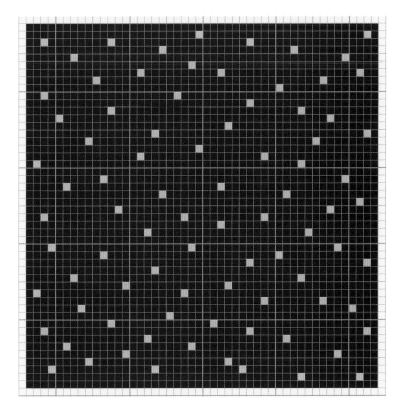

Bows and Rings Bridal Cushion

This little cushion was designed to hold the wedding rings during the marriage service. I have used slightly unconventional colours here but these can be changed to co-ordinate with the bride's bouquet, the flowers in the church and the bridesmaids' dresses. I have worked the design on a fine 14 hole canvas using woollen yarn but it can easily be stitched in stranded cotton to give a silky effect.

Materials

Anchor tapisserie wool:
  I skein 9556
  I skein 9524
  I skein 8396
  I skein 8006
  I skein 9094
  I skein 9076
  I skein 8686
  I skein 8264
  2 skeins 8602
Short length of gold diadem thread 300
One piece of 14 hole interlock canvas
  size 20 x 20 cm (8 x 8 in)
Backing fabric
Polyester toy stuffing

Instructions

1   Follow the chart to work the design, starting from the middle. Use half cross stitch throughout.

2   Press the embroidery on the back with a hot steam iron over a damp cloth and gently pull it back into shape.

3   With the right sides together, sew the backing fabric to the embroidery, starting one third of the way along the bottom edge of the cushion. Sew around the four sides, leaving a large gap to stuff the cushion. Trim the excess canvas and fabric.

4   Turn the cushion right side out.

5   Stuff with polyester toy stuffing and carefully sew up the gap.

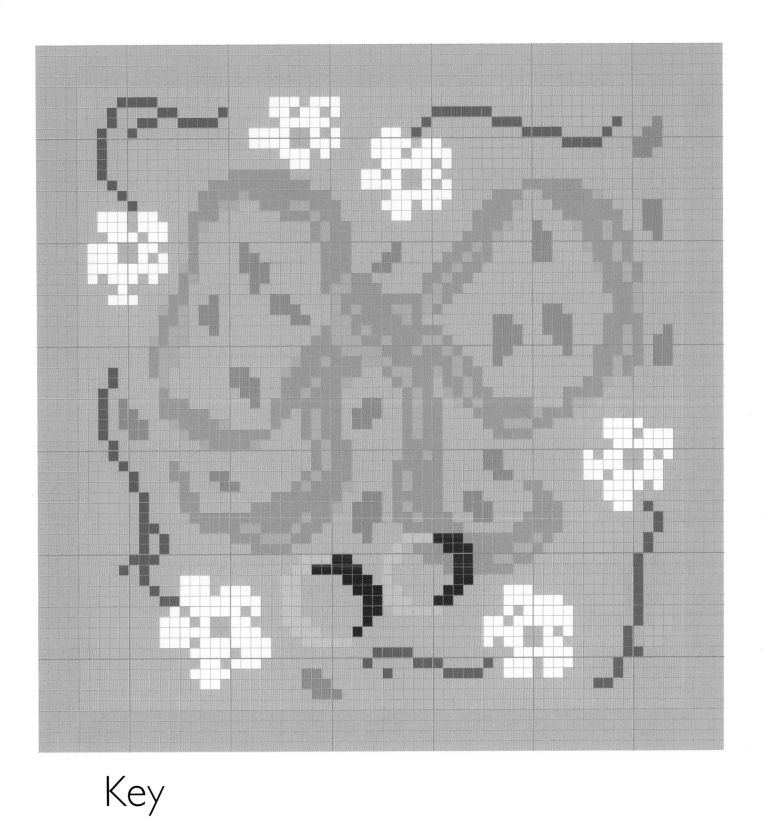

Key

Anchor tapisserie wool:

9556	9076	Gold diadem 300		
9524	8686			
8396	8264			
8006	8602			
9094				

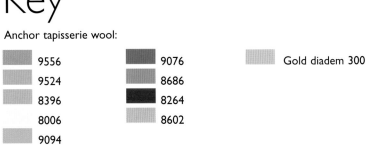

Christmas Decorations

Christmas decorations are quick to stitch and they can be done at any time in the year – not just at the last minute! These four little decorations are great fun to hang on a tree. I have used gold and silver thread to add sparkle and have oversewn on the background needlepoint the musical notes on the bell design and the star edging around the cross. Each design is worked twice to make a front and back panel. You could also adapt these designs for use as little pouches for small gifts simply by lining each side and leaving the top open.

Materials

Anchor tapisserie wool:
    1 skein 9102
    1 skein 8166
    1 skein 8490
    1 skein 8202
    1 skein 9510
    1 skein 9600
    1 skein 8644
1 reel gold diadem thread 300
1 reel silver diadem thread 301
Two pieces of 12 hole interlock canvas
    size 30 x 30 cm (12 x 12 in)
Polyester toy stuffing
Coloured ribbons

Instructions

1   Follow the charts to work the designs, starting from the middle of each. Use half cross stitch throughout. Use one piece of canvas to work the fronts and the other to work the backs of each piece.

2   Press the pieces of embroidery on the back with a hot steam iron over a damp cloth and gently pull them back into shape. Cut out each embroidery, ensuring that the corners are cut at an angle.

3   Fold the unworked canvas to the wrong side. Hold the front and back edges together with the right sides on the outside. Stitch the two pieces of canvas together, using a long-armed cross stitch, starting one third of the way along the bottom edge and working around the four sides. Leave a small gap to stuff the decoration.

4   Stuff each decoration with the toy stuffing and close the gap with long-armed cross stitch.

5   Sew a loop at the top with the coloured ribbon.

Key

Anchor tapisserie wool:

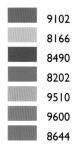

9102

8166

8490

8202

9510

9600

8644

Gold diadem 300

Silver diadem 301

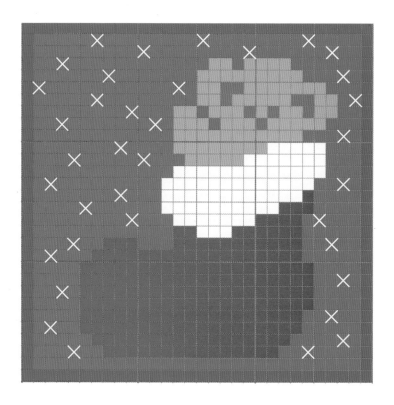

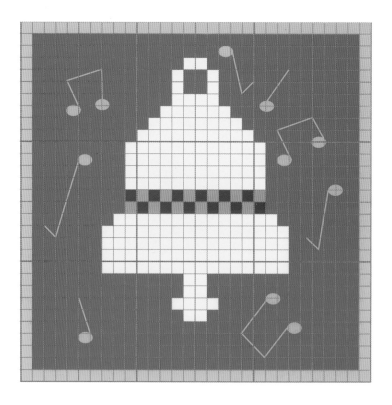

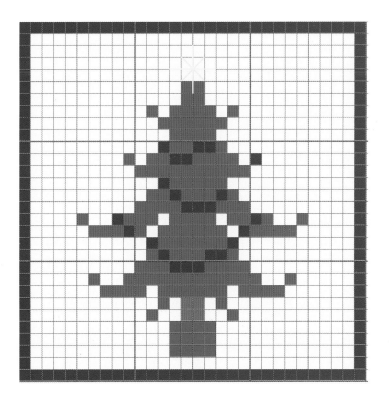

Conversion Chart

All the projects are worked using Anchor Tapestry Wools and threads. If you convert the colours to Appletons or DMC you may find a slight change in the finished result.

The conversion chart shown here gives a reference for the nearest DMC and Appletons colour for the Anchor range. In some cases there is not an exact match and it may be advisable to put all the suggested wool colours together for the particular design you intend stitching to ensure they sit together well. You may find you will have to alter some of the colours but you can ask advice directly from DMC and Appletons (see List of Suppliers, page 94).

Anchor	DMC	Appletons	Anchor	DMC	Appletons
8036	7905	871	8392	7200	752
8056	7745	471	8394	7132	753
8062	7846	691			
8006	ecru	871	8490	7153	803
8016	7078	552			
8014	7905	551	8434	7001	943
8038	7503	851	8486	7255	801
8052	7905	851			
8058	7058	473	8524	7253	602
			8592	7022	104
8156	7051	556	8526	7255	605
8136	7059	474			
8164	7439	626	8612	7245	896
8112	7078	551	8686	7028	821
8152	7918	861	8602	7021	891
8166	7052	864	8606	7019	893
8114	7431	552	8644	7798	821
			8634	7319	747
8264	7447	207			
8218	7544	503	8734	7594	321
8202	7666	502	8740	7591	926
8302	7121	621	8712	7568	461
8396	7202	754	8782	7027	561

Anchor	DMC	Appletons
8920	7861	521
8992	7914	437
8990	7909	436
9076	7370	642
9006	7386	404
9018	7384	402
9022	7385	407
9098	7771	424
9004	7042	402
9094	7382	541
9002	7604	401
9096	7772	422
9014	7402	401
9172	7422	541
9100	7042	425
9189	7890	406
9120	7386	428
9102	7043	426

Anchor	DMC	Appletons
9442	7171	701
9450	7845	303
9492	7059	301
9524	7455	861
9594	7460	202
9556	7918	863
9598	7063	123
9534	7919	862
9510	7166	204
9560	7446	721
9562	7178	722
9536	7919	477
9646	7938	187
9682	7238	934
9676	7232	931
9600	7168	126
9642	7468	305
9638	7162	122
9602	7169	126
9618	7215	221
9800	noir	993

List of Suppliers

All cushion pads, backing fabrics and cord can be found in good haberdashery shops. Upholstery fabrics work well for backing the cushions and suitable remnants can be found in large department stores such as John Lewis.

Appleton Brothers Ltd
Thames Works
Church Street
Chiswick
London W4 2PE
Tel: 0181 994 0711
Appleton wool (telephone for the nearest stockist).

CMP Habico Limited
Units B4-5
Wellington Road Industrial Estate,
Leeds
West Yorkshire LS 12 2UA
Tel: 0113 244 9810
Haberdashery supplies (telephone or write for nearest stockist).

Coats Crafts UK
PO Box 22
The Lingfield Estate
McMullen Road
Darlington
Co. Durham SL1 1TQ
Tel: 01325 365457
Anchor wool, stranded cottons and gold and silver diadem threads.

DMC Creative World Ltd
Pullman Road
Wigston
Leicester LE18 2DY
Tel: 0116 281 1040
Embroidery supplies, threads, linen.

Stella Edwards Needlework Designs
Barn Ldge
Kingshill Road
Four Ashes
High Wycombe
Bucks HP15 6LH
Tel: 01494 711650
Needlepoint kits (mail order, send a stamp-addressed envelope).

John Lewis
Oxford Street
London
Tel: 0171 629 7711
Extensive haberdashery department, large selection of cushion pads, including bolster and heart shape.

Ribbon Designs
42 Lake View
Edgware
Middlesex HA8 7RU
Tel: 0181 958 4966
Ribbons (mail order).

Shades at Mace & Nairn
89 Crane Street
Salisbury
Wiltshire SP1 2PY
Tel: 01722 336903
Appleton wools and embroidery specialists.

Spinning Jenny
Bradle
Keighley
West Yorkshire BD20 9DD
Tel: 01535 632469
Appleton wool (mail-order).

WHI Tapestry Shop Ltd
85 Pimlico Road
London SW1W 8PH
Tel: 0171 730 5366
Appleton wool (mail-order).

Index